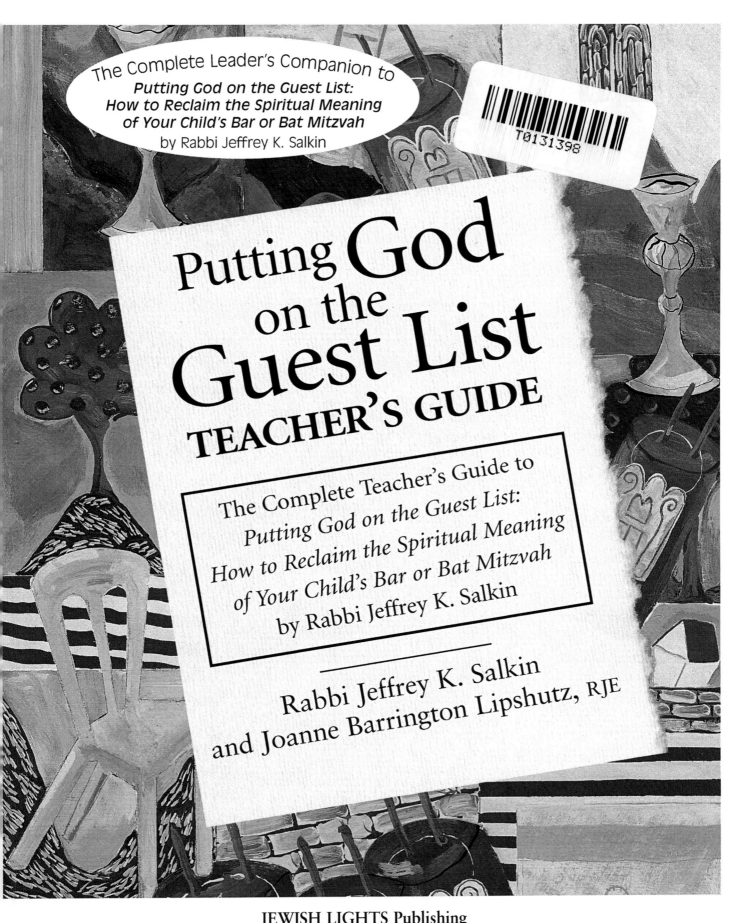

The Complete Leader's Companion to
*Putting God on the Guest List:
How to Reclaim the Spiritual Meaning
of Your Child's Bar or Bat Mitzvah*
by Rabbi Jeffrey K. Salkin

Putting God on the Guest List
TEACHER'S GUIDE

The Complete Teacher's Guide to
*Putting God on the Guest List:
How to Reclaim the Spiritual Meaning
of Your Child's Bar or Bat Mitzvah*
by Rabbi Jeffrey K. Salkin

Rabbi Jeffrey K. Salkin
and Joanne Barrington Lipshutz, RJE

JEWISH LIGHTS Publishing
Woodstock, Vermont

Putting God on the Guest List Teacher's Guide

2005 First Printing
© 2005 by Rabbi Jeffrey K. Salkin and Joanne Barrington Lipshutz

10   9   8   7   6   5   4   3   2   1

Manufactured in the United States of America

Published by Jewish Lights Publishing
A Division of LongHill Partners, Inc.
Sunset Farm Offices, Route 4, P.O. Box 237
Woodstock, VT 05091
Tel: (802) 457-4000 Fax: (802) 457-4004
www.jewishlights.com

Contents

Introduction

The spirituality of bar and bat mitzvah is not only one of the great challenges in the contemporary Jewish world—it is also one of the great challenges in synagogue educational programming. The big question is: How can we teach families to have a deeper appreciation of the bar and bat mitzvah experience so that the entire journey of bar and bat mitzvah can make a real difference in their lives?

From the time its first edition was published in 1992, *Putting God on the Guest List: How to Reclaim the Spiritual Meaning of Your Child's Bar or Bat Mitzvah* has made a real difference in the lives of its readers. In this teacher's guide, an experienced Jewish educator and a rabbi (who is also the author of *Putting God on the Guest List*) suggest lesson plans, activities, and discussion triggers for many of the book's chapters. In general, the activities in this guide should take between thirty-five and fifty minutes to complete.

We hope these suggestions will help you bring new life to the important discussion of how to keep spirit in this life-cycle event, teaching both young people and parents how they might truly put God on the guest list.

Remember, you can also use *For Kids: Putting God on Your Guest List*, the students' version of *Putting God on the Guest List*, and its companion book, *The Bar/Bat Mitzvah Memory Book: An Album for Treasuring the Spiritual Celebration* (both Jewish Lights), as part of your program. These resources can be used effectively with both students and parents, and have discussion questions built right into their pages. It would be helpful for parents to have the adult version and for students to have the kids' version, so that the material can be studied on a level appropriate to the reader.

Please note: All page references in this teacher's guide are to the third edition of *Putting God on the Guest List: How to Reclaim the Spiritual Meaning of Your Child's Bar or Bat Mitzvah*.

1

Beyond "Today I Am a Man"

THE LURE OF LORE
(An Activity for Parents and Kids)

Summary

This exercise explores the lore of bar/bat mitzvah. Participants will encounter various midrashim on why bar/bat mitzvah is at the age of thirteen.

Before You Begin, You Need

- A copy of the midrash on page 7 for each participant

- A copy of the age-appropriate discussion questions on page 8–9 for each group

- A pen or pencil for each participant

Doing the Activity

1. Read to the group the activity opening text on p. 6.

2. Divide the participants into four groups of parents and four groups of kids.

3. Give each group a copy of the midrash on p. 7 and the appropriate set of discussion questions. Parent groups should get the parent version on p. 8; kid groups should get the kids version on p. 9.

4. Ask the groups to read and discuss the midrash and each of the discussion questions. Depending on the number of participants in your group, this step should take about a half hour.

5. Gather the groups together and compare answers from parents and kids. How are they alike? How are they different?

6. Bring the activity to an end with a discussion of the closing question on p. 6.

Opening Words

Why is bar and bat mitzvah at the age of thirteen? Tradition, puberty? Let's ask the ancient Rabbis, who created that great form of literature, midrash—the Jewish art of telling stories about things that happen in the Bible.

> Most references to the significance of the age of thirteen come from stories the Rabbis told about characters in the Bible. Those stories constitute the body of Jewish interpretive literature known as midrash. It was the way that the Rabbis continually breathed new life into the text of Torah and found new meanings within its stories. (*Putting God on the Guest List*, p. 5)

Closing Question

> As these midrashim have shown, kids are making important decisions at bar/bat mitzvah age that will affect the rest of their lives—and the life of the Jewish community. How can we help them become Jewish adults?

Midrash—Abram in the Idol Store

Abraham's father, Terach, is in the idol business in Ur, a city in ancient Sumer. He goes away on business and leaves his thirteen-year-old son, Abram, in charge of the idol shop. Abram, who is later called Abraham, shatters all the idols in the store with a stick and then places the stick in the hand of the largest idol. When Terach gets back, he sees the ruined merchandise.

"What happened?" Terach demands.

"Oh, father, it was terrible," says Abram. "The small idols got hungry and started fighting for food. Then the large idol got angry and broke the smaller ones into little pieces. It was frightening. I don't want to talk about it."

"Wait a second," says Terach. "Idols don't get hungry. They don't get angry. They don't speak. They're just ... they're just clay idols."

"So," Abram asks with a smile, "why do you worship them?"

Questions for Parent Discussion

1. What idols would you hope your adolescent might smash in his or her life?

2. A midrash says that, at the age of thirteen, the twins Jacob and Esau went their separate ways: Jacob to the worship of God, and Esau to idolatry, each following his own true nature and inclinations. What choices can Jewish children today make when they become bar or bat mitzvah?

3. The Talmud says that Bezalel, the namesake of the famous art school in Jerusalem, was thirteen when he designed the ancient tabernacle for worship in the wilderness.

   What could emerging Jewish adults build in their lives today?

4. According to the Midrash, Moses's parents, Amram and Yocheved, decided to live apart in Egypt because they did not want to bring any more children into a world of slavery and oppression. Their daughter, Miriam, convinced them to get back together. "This is wrong!" she said to her parents. "By refusing to live together and to have any more children, you are depriving our people of a future!" One source says that Miriam was five years old when she stood up for what she believed in, even though it could have gotten her in trouble. But as a parent, it's easy to suspect that she might have been closer to thirteen at the time.

   How would you like your child to be inspired by Miriam?

Questions for Kid Discussion

1. What idols do you want to smash? (Hint: An idol is not just a false god that might be made of wood or stone. It is anything that people think is very, very important, but turns out not to be—or anything that people worship that isn't worthy of being worshiped. Think about the expression "teen idol.")

2. A midrash says that, at the age of thirteen, the twins Jacob and Esau went their separate ways: Jacob to the worship of God, and Esau to idolatry, each following his own true nature and inclinations.

   What important choices can you make about how you live your life when you become bar or bat mitzvah?

3. The Talmud says that Bezalel, the namesake of the famous art school in Jerusalem, was thirteen when he designed the ancient tabernacle for worship in the wilderness.

   What can you and other emerging Jewish adults build in your lives?

4. According to the Midrash, Moses's parents, Amram and Yocheved, decided to live apart in Egypt because they did not want to bring any more children into a world of slavery and oppression. Their daughter, Miriam, convinced them to get back together. "This is wrong!" she said to them. "By refusing to live together and to have any more children, you are depriving our people of a future!" One source says that Miriam was five years old when she stood up for what she believed in, even though it could have gotten her in trouble. But as a young adult, it's easy to suspect that she might have been closer to thirteen years old at the time.

   Have you ever stood up for something you believe in, like Miriam did? Is there anything you think it's important for young Jewish adults to speak out against today?

TEEN IDOL SMASHER
(An Activity for Parents and Kids)

Summary

This activity explores from many angles the famous story of Abram breaking his father's idols. It invites critical thinking about what the story means to us today and the importance of struggle throughout Jewish history.

Before You Begin, You Need

- A copy of the midrash on p. 7 for each participant
- Several sheets of paper and a pen or pencil for each participant

Doing the Activity

1. Read to the group the activity opening text on p. 11.

2. Hand out pencils and paper.

3. Ask participants to write down their answers to the discussion questions for part one on p. 11.

4. Facilitate open discussion and general sharing about the participants' responses.

5. Explain to the group that they're not alone in fighting with their parent or child—arguments between the generations are a major part of Judaism. One of the most famous examples of this is found in the legend of Abraham and Terach.

6. Give a copy of the midrash on page 7 to each participant.

7. Read the midrash aloud and discuss as a group the questions for part two on p. 11–12. Open the floor to questions and general discussion.

8. Bring the activity to an end with a discussion of the closing question on p. 11.

Opening Words

I'm sure no one here has ever had a fight or disagreement with their kid or with their parent, so this exercise may seem really strange to you. Today we are going to use a well-known legend to help us talk about communication between parents and kids as we reach the age of bar and bat mitzvah.

Closing Question

How is this ancient legend relevant to our lives today?

Questions for Discussion—Part One

1. What was the nature of the last argument or disagreement you had with your teen or parent?

2. Now, what do you think it was *really* about? (For example, he or she doesn't listen; he or she doesn't take me seriously; he or she doesn't know where I'm coming from; and so on.)

3. What words or phrases do you often find yourself using when you get into arguments or disagreements with your teen or parent?

4. What words or phrases do you think the other person often uses when you get into arguments or disagreements with them?

5. How did your last argument end? Do you think the same problem will come up again?

6. How did you feel after the argument?

7. How do you think the other person felt afterward?

Questions for Discussion—Part Two

1. What were Abram and Terach really fighting about? *(Teacher's Tip: Abram started this argument in order to create the ultimate break with idolatry.)*

2. What was Terach's primary reason for getting involved in this argument? *(Teacher's Tip: His merchandise. Rabbi Lawrence Kushner once asked, satirically: "Did Terach have insurance on his stuff? Was it covered?")*

3. What was Abram's motivation for starting this argument? *(Teacher's Tip: What he believed to be the truth about God and Terach's clay idols.)*

4. How did Abram win this argument? *(Teacher's Tip: He won by using his wits to force Terach to realize that his clay idols were useless. If Abram had simply told his father this, rather than showing him, Abram probably wouldn't have convinced Terach to see his point of view.)*

5. The legend you learned as a kid isn't the only story about Abram and his dad's store. Here's another: An old woman comes into the store (let's call it "Gods 'R' Us!") to buy an idol.

Abram asks her: "How old are you?" She replies: "Seventy years old." Abram says to her: "Why would you buy an idol that was made only last week and worship it?" She goes away without buying a thing. What message do you think this story was meant to convey? *(Teacher's Tip: Consumerism can lead to buying things you don't need. As this god was a direct representation of the physical world, the story also exemplifies a willingness to look only at the surface of things, rather than searching for deeper meanings. Some people lack the imagination and the ability— or desire—to see the more profound things that aren't right in front of them.)*

6. Here's another legend about Terach's idol store: A man comes in and wants to buy a god that looks just like him. When he can't find one, he walks out. What do you think this story was meant to convey? *(Teacher's Tip: That some people only worship themselves.)*

7. Here's another scene that didn't make it into the childhood version of the "Gods 'R' Us" legend. After Abram smashes his father's idols, Terach takes him to King Nimrod. Nimrod sentences Abram to death and throws him into a furnace. An angel comes and saves Abram. Do you think this part of the story is a coming attraction for other things in Jewish history? *(Teacher's Tip: Jews have suffered time and time again for their beliefs—particularly during the Spanish Inquisition and the Holocaust.)*

Bar/Bat Mitzvah Family Feud
(An Activity for Parents and Kids)

Summary

This program encourages parents and young people to consider how bar/bat mitzvah can change kids' lives. This could turn into a planning session for future synagogue youth and educational programs, as the community discusses the preparation of its young adults to truly become bar and bat mitzvah—mature enough to do *mitzvot*.

Before You Begin, You Need

- A sheet of paper for each participant marked with columns, one labeled, "What changes in your life at bar and bat mitzvah?" and the other labeled, "What stays the same in your life after bar and bat mitzvah?"

- A pencil or pen for each participant

Doing the Activity

1. Read to the group the activity opening text on p. 13.

2. Divide parents and kids into small groups.

3. Distribute the two-column answer sheets.

4. Without discussion, each participant should create a list of items for each column—what in your life changes at bar/bat mitzvah, and what stays the same.

5. Each group should appoint a spokesperson. Group members should then compare their lists. How do the kids' lists differ from the adults' lists?

6. Reassemble into a large group and discuss. Each group's spokesperson should summarize his or her group's observations. What patterns do you detect?

7. Bring the activity to an end with a discussion of the closing questions on p. 14.

Opening Words

[Most] Jewish parents need to turn inward at bar and bat mitzvah time and ask themselves these thorny questions: "Why are we doing this? What does it all mean?" I have discovered that many parents and children have never discussed the meaning of bar and bat mitzvah with each other. What results is a ceremony that is essentially a performance, a demonstration of rudimentary linguistic competence in an ancient language. Scant attention is paid to its underlying meaning and beauty.

Yet, one thread links all the bar and bat mitzvah ceremonies throughout history, all the comings of age of every Jewish boy from Abraham on and of every Jewish girl from Sarah on. Bar mitzvah and bat mitzvah are a passage, but not one of puberty. "It's when I become a man," say too many bar mitzvah candidates. Curiously, bat mitzvah girls rarely say, "It's when I become a woman." Instead, they say, "Bat mitzvah is when I get new responsibilities." And they are right.

Bar and bat mitzvah is about ritual maturity. It is about growing up as a Jew. It is about becoming a fuller member of the Jewish community. But it is also about moral responsibility, about connecting to Torah, to community, to God. (*Putting God on the Guest List*, p. 18)

Bar and bat mitzvah is a celebration of the changes that happen in our kids' lives—in terms of Judaism and in other ways as well. We're going to divide up parents and kids into small groups and ask two questions: What changes in your life at the time of bar/bat mitzvah? What stays the same?

Closing Questions

For the kids: What's one thing you wish that your parents would understand about you?

For the parents: How can we help our kids to mature as young Jews?

2

"Speak to the Children of Israel": How Bar and Bat Mitzvah Speak to the Inner Life of Children

DON'T LET DOWN THE COACH*
(An Activity for Parents and Kids)

* This activity is also appropriate for Chapter Four—"Hearing God's Voice: The Meaning of Torah."

Summary

This is a fun game about how the Rabbis envisioned the transmission of tradition and our role in it.

Before You Begin, You Need

- A space large enough for your whole group to move around in freely

- A cassette or CD player and some popular Jewish music, such as songs by Rick Recht, Craig Taubman, Doug Cotler, Debbie Friedman, Kol B'Seder, or Danny Maseng. Cue up a few two- or three-minute songs that convey a message about tradition.

- Decide if you have enough kids and parents—total—for four groups. (Ideally, each group will be made up of no more than ten players.) Otherwise, you'll need to break your participants into however many even groups you can fill with an even number of players: two, four, six, and so on.

- A soup spoon for each participant

- A tennis ball for each group, with a meaningful term written on each of them—e.g., Torah, Talmud, Hebrew, mitzvah, prayer, holiness, freedom, justice, or Shabbat

- Prizes for the fastest team (optional)

Doing the Activity

1. Read to the group the activity opening text on pp. 16–17.

2. Break your players into the previously decided even number of groups. Each group should include both adults and kids.

3. Send each group to a different area in the room. Each group should form a line facing another group across a sizable distance—large enough to make a relay race credible and fun.

4. Distribute spoons and tennis balls: Each individual must have a spoon; each group must have a tennis ball.

5. Each person with a tennis ball should read aloud the term written on it and think about what the term means to him or her. He or she should place the ball in his or her spoon. (Remind participants that while speed is important, really thinking about the term on each ball is key!)

6. When the music starts, the game begins. Each ball should be delivered—spoon to spoon—to the person at the front of the line on the facing group. If the ball drops, the person who dropped it must figure out how to scoop it up with his or her spoon. No hands allowed!

7. The ball's recipient must read aloud the term on the ball they've been passed, think about what it means to him or her, and then deliver the ball to the next person in line across the room. Once their tennis ball has been successfully transferred, this person should join the end of the line.

8. Continue this process as long as the song you've chosen continues to play. When the song stops, the fastest team is the one that has gotten its tennis balls the farthest down the line.

9. Bring the activity to an end with a discussion of the closing questions on p. 17.

Opening Words

In the Midrash (*Kohelet Rabbah* 12:10) ... we read: "The words of the wise are like a young girl's ball. As a ball is flung by hand without falling, so Moses received the Torah at Sinai and delivered it to Joshua, Joshua to the elders, the elders to the prophets, and the prophets delivered it to the Great Synagogue."

That is how the ancient Rabbis imagined the *shalshelet ha-kabbalah,* the great chain of tradition, that went from generation to generation: As a ball that is tossed, playfully, from teacher to student.

Once, ... at a place called Mount Sinai, the Coach gathered us together, saying, "OK, you, Cohen, Schwartz, Goldberg, even you, O'Malley (whose descendants will someday join the Jewish people through conversion). Here's the plan. Go out for the long pass.

I throw the ball to you, you catch it, then throw it to your kids, who will throw it to their kids. That is how the ball gets passed from generation to generation."

The ball has gone from Israel to Spain to Germany to Poland to Russia to Northern Africa. We know the names of some of the ball throwers: Moses, Aaron, Deborah, David, Miriam, Ruth, Rabbi Akiba, Beruriah, Maimonides, Hannah Senesh, and Henrietta Szold. All of our ancestors had his or her own way of catching the ball, of running with it, and then throwing it. Certain generations fumbled the ball, and almost let it slip through their hands. But they never completely lost the ball.

Our generation won't drop the ball or fail to throw it to another generation. If we drop it, there are no guarantees it will bounce again into our hands so we can throw it to future generations. (*Putting God on the Guest List*, pp. 24–25)

There are many ways to think about the meaning of tradition in our lives. Bar and bat mitzvah are just two Jewish traditions out of many. What other ones do your families take part in?

Today we're going to play a game inspired by the Rabbis' simile that wisdom is like a little girl's ball, passed from one generation to another—with one small twist. The ball isn't thrown. It's carried on a spoon.

Closing Questions

1. Think about the game we just played. Who did your teammates represent? (*Teacher's Tip: They represented the Jewish People.*)

2. How big is this team? (*Teacher's Tip: It's very big, including all the Jews who are alive today, all the Jews who have ever been alive, and all the Jews who will ever be alive. We are a small people and a large family.*)

3. Do you have to like all your fellow team members? (*Teacher's Tip: No. That is probably rarely the case even on an athletic team. There is a mitzvah that governs relationships between Jews, though*—ahavat Yisrael, *love of the People Israel. We may not get along with all Jews, but* ahavat Yisrael *tells us that working together for the greater good of Judaism is always the right thing to do.*)

4. What are some ways that you can support your team members? (*Teacher's Tip: You could plant a tree in Israel by giving a donation to the Jewish National Fund, volunteer at a Mazon-approved hunger relief agency, or visit Jewish residents in your local nursing home.*)

5. Who is the Coach? (*Teacher's Tip: God is the Coach.*)

Here's another excerpt from *Putting God on the Guest List:*

> There are rules to this "game" of Judaism. *Number One:* Never forget that you are playing on a team that is larger than the people you see before you. It is a very, very big team. *Number Two:* Never let down your team members. You may not know them. If you do, you may not like some of them. But they need you, and you need them, for the ball to continue being passed through the generations. *Number Three:* Never let down the Coach. (*Putting God on the Guest List,* p. 25)

Questions for Discussion

1. What were some of the terms that you read on the tennis balls?

2. What did they make you think about? Did any particular memories or goals come to mind?

3. What were you thinking as you delivered the ball to the next person?

4. Was anyone afraid of dropping the ball? Why?

5. Sometimes the tennis balls went from parents to kids, and sometimes from kids to parents. What might this mean? *(Teacher's Tip: Traditions are sometimes passed from older people to younger ones, but the opposite can happen, too. Jewish summer camps have shown this very effectively:* havdalah *services first became popular there, and Tisha B'Av was rescued from relative obscurity by them.)*

6. You only had a few minutes to try to get the ball to the end of the line. How is that similar to the transmission of Judaism? How is it different?

7. What did you learn today about passing traditions back and forth between the generations?

3

The River of Tears: How Bar and Bat Mitzvah Speak to the Inner Lives of Parents and Grandparents

YOU WERE THERE

(An Activity for Grandparents, Parents, and Kids)

Summary

This activity is a light one. Using a fun talk show format, it shows how bar and bat mitzvah has both changed and stayed the same over the years.

Before You Begin, You Need

- Chairs for all participants, set up in talk show–style—two chairs facing a bank of chairs for the audience

- Someone—a teacher, cantor, rabbi, or program director—to act as the talk show host and interviewer

- A few parents and grandparents to act as interviewees

Doing the Activity

1. Read to the group the activity opening text on p. 20.

2. The interviewer asks questions as if he or she is the host of a talk show, feeling free to have fun and interact with the interviewee. (See the discussion questions on p. 20 for a list of potential interview questions.)

3. As the interview winds down, the "host" should briefly summarize what has been said, talking about general patterns or any especially interesting pieces of information.

4. Open the floor to questions about the interview from other participants.

5. Repeat the process until each of the designated interviewees has been interviewed.

6. Bring the activity to an end with a discussion of the closing questions on below.

Opening Words

This activity is called "You Were There." Today, we are going to interview parents and grandparents about their bar and bat mitzvah experiences.

Questions for Discussion

1. Where and when did you celebrate your bar/bat mitzvah?

2. What was going on in the world then?

3. In what synagogue did your ceremony take place? What kind of synagogue was it?

4. Do you remember the name of the rabbi? The cantor? Any of your teachers?

5. What was your Torah portion? Your *haftarah* portion?

6. What do you remember about the service?

7. What memories do you have of the celebration? Did you get any special gifts? Do you still have any of them?

Following this activity could be an excellent opportunity to distribute *Putting God on the Guest List's* companion memory book, *The Bar/Bat Mitzvah Memory Book: An Album for Treasuring the Spiritual Celebration.* It's an "instant heirloom"—allowing kids to record memories that will last a lifetime and can be shared with the next generation.

Closing Questions

The word *zachor*—"remember!"—is used as a commandment 169 times in the Torah. Does anyone know the square root of 169? It's 13!

What memories of the upcoming bar/bat mitzvah experience do you want your child or grandchild to have? What memories would you kids like to have of your bar/bat mitzvah celebrations?

THE LOMAN FAMILY PICNIC
(An Activity for Parents)

Summary

This can be quite a powerful program. It explores the upcoming bar and bat mitzvah as a connection with family members who have come before. It entails acting out an excerpt from a play by Pulitzer Prize–winning playwright Donald Margulies called *The Loman Family Picnic*. (Note: no memorization is required for this activity. In fact, it will be more effective if the participants are reading the material for the first time.)

Before You Begin, You Need

- A space large enough for the performance. A stage is not necessary, but there should be enough room for your audience and actors.

- A copy of the excerpt from *The Loman Family Picnic* on pp. 23 and 25 for each participant. Scene one should be on one side of the handout and scene two on the other.

Doing the Activity

1. Read to the group the activity opening text on p. 22.

2. Distribute one copy of *The Loman Family Picnic* excerpt to each participant.

3. Find three volunteers: one to read the part of Stewie, a bar mitzvah aged boy; one to read the part of Doris, his mother; and one to read the part of Herbie, his father.

4. Let the play begin!

5. When the first scene has been read, invite discussion of the questions on p. 24. Continue by reading scene two and exploring the discussion questions about it on p. 26.

6. Bring the activity to an end with a discussion of the closing question on p. 22.

Opening Words

Personal immortality is the unspoken, unarticulated prayer at every life-cycle event. The prolific Talmudic scholar Rabbi Jacob Neusner spoke for many of us when he wrote, "At a bar or a bat mitzvah, a parent thinks not so much of the future as of the past, especially if a grandparent or a parent is deceased; the entire family one has known has assembled, and that is as much the past as the future."

At some level, often one that is deep and unspoken, we know this. I remember a particular bat mitzvah in my last congregation. The father of the bat mitzvah had never struck me as a particularly emotional man, but at that service, standing over the Torah, he wept profusely. Standing next to him at the reading table, I was bewildered. Weeks later, he told me why he had cried:

"My father and my brother are both deceased. My kids are named for both of them. And now my daughters are both mature Jewish adults. I felt that the cycle was complete. Certain things touch you that persuade you of a Higher Power. For me, it was the memory of people who had died. I tell you, I could hear them taking pleasure in my daughter reading the Torah." (*Putting God on the Guest List*, p. 33)

Today we're going to act out an excerpt from a play called *The Loman Family Picnic* by the Pulitzer Prize–winning playwright Donald Margulies. You may recognize the name Loman from the classic play *Death of a Salesman* by Arthur Miller. Margulies's play is sort of a midrash on it, telling a similar story from a different point of view. In *The Loman Family Picnic,* a family is preparing for their older son's bar mitzvah. We're going to watch two scenes from it unfold—but please, only read scene one now. We will get to scene two later.

Closing Question

How can we, as parents and as synagogue members, ensure that the new generation of Jewish adults experience meaningful, spiritually powerful bar/bat mitzvah celebrations?

Scene One

Stewie: "Tell me what I'm reading," I said. "Tell me what the words mean." He looks at me like I'm not speaking any known language. "What does it mean?!," I said. "What am I saying?!" "What does it matter?" he says, "you can read it." "Yeah, but what does it mean?!" "It means you will be bar mitzvah!," he says. "But the words don't mean anything to me, they're just these funny little sounds." "Those funny sounds," he says, "are what make a boy different from a Jew!" "So?! You taught me how to read but you didn't teach me how to understand! What kind of Jew is that?!" This does not go over big. His lips are turning blue. I think he's gonna have an angina attack. All he cares about is rolling out bar mitzvah boys to re-populate the earth. We look the part and we can sing, but we don't know what we're saying! I have had it!

Doris: You have to go through with your bar mitzvah, Stewie.

Stewie: You don't know what it's like, Ma, day after day of this. I'm being brainwashed.

Doris: You're just getting cold feet. You'll be fine.

Stewie: I can't do it, Ma.

Doris (*infuriated, through gritted teeth*): How dare you do this to me!

Stewie (*also through gritted teeth*): What? What am I doing to you?!

Doris: You know how hard I've been working to make you a beautiful party?!

Stewie: Me? It's not for me. Make your beautiful party! I just won't be there. Tell everybody I got the runs!

Doris: Don't do this to me, Stewie! Don't make me cancel! We'll lose all our deposits! Is that what you want?! Hm?! Your father's blood money down the drain?! The hall, the band, the flowers?! The caterers?! I already bought my dress, what do you want me to do with it? Hock it? I've spent days laying out response cards like solitaire and clipping tables together! This is no time to be a prima donna, Stewie. One more week. That's all I ask. Give me the nachas, then you can do whatever the hell you want. You want to renounce Judaism? Renounce Judaism. Become a monk, I don't care.

Stewie (*teeth gritted again*): Remember, Ma, I'm doing this for you. I'll go through with it, and sing nice, and make you proud, and make the relatives cry, but once I'm bar mitzvahed, that's it, Ma, I'm never stepping foot in that place. Never again.

Doris: Thank you, darling, thank you.

Questions for Discussion—Scene One

1. What are Stewie's complaints about the bar mitzvah process?

2. What doesn't he like about learning Hebrew?

3. What doesn't Stewie like about his teacher?

4. What is the only thing he thinks his teacher cares about?

5. If you were on a religious school committee, how would you try to fix Stewie's situation?

6. What would bring more meaning to the bar mitzvah for Stewie?

7. Why is Doris so eager for him to become bar mitzvah?

8. What are her priorities?

9. What do you think of the way Stewie talks about bar mitzvah—speaking of it as "bar mitzva-hed?" What does that grammar reveal about the nature of bar mitzvah to many young people and families?

10. Does this remind anyone here of his or her own bar or bat mitzvah experiences?

11. How do you want your children's experiences to be different?

Scene Two

Stewie *(to the audience):* My friend Jeffrey cleared twenty-two hundred dollars at his bar mitzvah. And his was smaller than this. I'm gonna buy an electric guitar and an amp, and a bunch of CDs. I made a list last week in back of my science notebook. Twenty-two hundred bucks; that's a lot of CDs.

Herbie *(to us):* She wanted a big party? *(He shrugs)* Alright, we'll have a big party. You want tuxedos? We'll rent tuxedos. Then you have to buy shoes to go with the tuxedos for me and the boys. And a fancy French razor cut, 'cause a regular haircut wouldn't look right with a tux.

Doris: It just wouldn't.

Herbie: And a dress for her—alright, it's gorgeous, but still, aren't we going a little overboard here?

Doris: This is an *event*. A big deal. There's no cutting corners when you're putting together an event like this. You go all out, or why bother? Oh, look … people are starting to arrive. I don't believe it, look who's here. You know how I told you about Hitler murdering the Jews? Well there's Grandma's uncle Izzy. The one who died in the war.

Stewie: Where?

Doris: The one in the striped pajamas. *(Calls)* Uncle Izzy! Go into the smorgasbord! You must be starving! *(Blows a kiss)* … Did you see who he was with? Cousin Rifka. Remember I told you … about the Triangle Factory fire? Poor thing.

Questions for Discussion—Scene Two

1. How does Herbie react to the preparations for his son's bar mitzvah?

2. What do you think he's really thinking and feeling?

3. Doris imagines that she sees departed relatives at the bar mitzvah celebration. How did those relatives die? What is the significance of their deaths? *(Teacher's Tip: The Triangle Factory fire was a tragic event in American history. A group of immigrant women, most of them Jews, died during a fire in a crowded garment factory in New York City in 1911. The disaster inspired a small revolution in labor laws.)*

4. Why do you think those departed relatives were at Stewie's bar mitzvah celebration?

5. What might the victim of the Triangle Factory fire represent? *(Teacher's Tip: A memory of our working class origins in America, particularly at a time of affluence, is one possibility. This person may also represent the Jewish legacy of social justice.)*

6. Who is the person in the striped pajamas?

7. What might the Holocaust victim represent? *(Teacher's Tip: He may represent Jewish suffering or survival.)*

8. What is the irony in what Doris says to Grandma's uncle Izzy? *(Teacher's Tip: He really had been starving. Notice how we use that term nowadays—simply for someone who is a little hungry.)*

9. In what way are departed relatives present at a bar or bat mitzvah celebration? *(Teacher's Tip: Departed relatives are at bar/bat mitzvah celebrations in the memories of those in attendance. Also, by passing down rituals and traditions to subsequent generations, these people have influenced the lives of others, leaving their own unique stamp on Judaism as it is practiced by their friends and family.)*

10. In what way are Jews of the past at a bar mitzvah celebration? Jews of the present? Jews of the future? *(Teacher's Tip: They are present as links on the chain of Judaism, passing traditions along through thousands of years of history.)*

5

Putting the Mitzvah Back in Bar and Bat Mitzvah

INTERGALACTIC YAVNEH*
(An Activity for Parents and Kids)

* This activity is also appropriate for Chapter Four—"Hearing God's Voice: The Meaning of Torah."

Summary

By asking participants to decide which *mitzvot* are most important to carry on, this activity is a way for kids and parents to think about the future of Judaism.

Before You Begin, You Need

- A sheet of paper for each participant, marked with the list of *mitzvot* on p. 30

- A pencil or pen for each participant

- A "space helmet" or other intergalactic costume for the teacher (optional)

Doing the Activity

1. Read to the group the activity opening text on p. 28.

2. Break into groups of ten. Each group should include both parents and kids.

3. Hand out the previously prepared sheets of intergalactic *mitzvot* possibilities.

4. Explain to participants that their task is to decide the seven Jewish practices that should survive—and why. Allow about thirty minutes for this exercise.

5. Gather all the groups and discuss which *mitzvot* the participants chose to keep and why. Which would still be relevant? Which would be irrelevant? Are there ways to make even those "irrelevant" *mitzvot* relevant again?

6. Bring the activity to an end with a discussion of the closing question on pp. 28–29.

Opening Words

Jewish children become bar or bat mitzvah because of God's Covenant with the people of Israel. The *mitzvot* are our end of the covenant. *Mitzvah*, in fact, is one of the most important ideas Judaism gave to the world: A relationship with God entails mutual responsibility. Traditionally, there are 613 *mitzvot* derived from the Torah. Ritual *mitzvot*, such as observing Shabbat and keeping the dietary laws of *kashrut*, connect us to God. Ethical *mitzvot*, such as not murdering or gossiping, govern our relationship with people. Some *mitzvot* are in positive language: "Thou *shalt* ..." Others are in negative language: "Thou shalt *not* ..." The idea of *mitzvah* is central to Jewish identity. It is the essence of the Covenant, our end of the agreement made at Sinai, the summit of Jewish existence. (*Putting God on the Guest List*, p. 61)

In the first century C.E., the Romans destroyed the Jewish Temple and Jerusalem. A group of sages escaped from the city and met in Yavneh, an Israeli town. There, they sat around and determined what the future of Judaism would be. The sages worked together to decide what parts of Judaism could stay the same, even without the Temple and the Jewish city of Jerusalem, and what parts would need to change. They figured out what books would be included in the Hebrew Bible, what the liturgy would be like, and that Passover would be celebrated in people's homes, rather than in the Temple as it had been before the Temple's destruction.

Welcome to Intergalactic Yavneh. The year is 2440. Invaders from the evil galaxy of Treifonia have decimated the earth. Luckily, millions of people have managed to escape to other planets in other galaxies. Using sophisticated radio technology—actually, their Blackberries—about a million Jews who have survived locate each other in the wilds of space. They agree to find unoccupied planets and settle on them, creating Jewish planets. After a lot of searching, they discover _____ [number of groups you will have] genuinely uninhabited planets. At each planet, the Jews hold a conference. Its purpose? To determine which Jewish *mitzvot* are still necessary and possible to carry out, even away from planet Earth.

Like the sages at Yavneh, their purpose—no, *your* purpose—is to re-create Judaism.

Closing Question

Well, friends, we may not be intergalactic Jews. At least not yet. But one thing is for sure: In every age, Jews have interpreted and reinterpreted Judaism and its traditions in new ways. Can you think of any new interpretations that have changed Judaism in your lifetime? (*Teacher's Tip: Women were first ordained as rabbis only in the end of the twentieth century.*)

The [Torah] scroll lets us hear God speak, either with hushed, comforting quiet or with a great cosmic peal that humbles. It is the way we hear God. It is the way we stand at Sinai once again. All that the Jewish people have been and all that we will be is on the *bimah* as a youth reads from the scroll. It is a scroll that has been battered and burned and torn through the ages. But it has survived because the Jewish people have cherished it.

The Talmud puts it this way: "We were sitting and discussing the Torah, going from the Torah to the Prophets, and from the Prophets to the Writings, until the words became as radiant as when they were first imparted at Sinai" (Palestinian Talmud, Hagigah 2:1). That is how studying Torah can be for us as well—a moment of feeling the radiance that our ancestors felt when they first stood at Sinai and received the words for the first time. (*Putting God on the Guest List*, p. 58)

Intergalactic *Mitzvot* Possibilities

- Keeping kosher

- Shabbat

- *Pesach* (Passover)

- *Hachnasat orchim* (showing hospitality)

- *Ahavat ha-ger* (loving the stranger)

- Studying Torah

- Worship

- *Mezuzot* on houses

- *Tzedakah* (sacred giving)

- Learning Hebrew

- *Teshuvah* (turning inward and fixing yourself)

- *Tzaar baalei chayim* (kindness to other living creatures)

- Sukkot

- Loyalty to the land of Israel

6

Rites and Wrongs of Passage: Putting the Party in Perspective

THE TEN COMMANDMENTS OF BAR/BAT MITZVAH
(An Activity for Parents and Kids)

Summary

This activity uses Jewish laws from medieval Europe to help kids and parents think about the ethics of celebration.

Before You Begin, You Need

- A photocopy of the sumptuary laws, or laws regulating personal expenditures, on pp. 33–34 for each participant

- Paper and a pencil or pen for each participant

- A white board or large pad of paper and easel

Doing the Activity

1. Read to the group the activity opening text on p. 32.

2. Hand out a copy of the sumptuary laws on p. 33–34 to each participant.

3. Read the laws as a group and discuss the questions on p. 35.

4. Break participants into small groups and invite them to write their own ten commandments for bar/bat mitzvah celebrations.

5. Allow twenty to twenty-five minutes for this exercise and reassemble participants into the larger group. Write down their ten commandments on the large pad of paper or white board, looking for common themes and any particularly interesting ideas.

6. Bring the activity to an end with a discussion of the closing question on p. 32.

Opening Words

Modern American Jews are not the first Jews to confront the ethical overtones of conspicuous consumption. Even in medieval times, there were excesses in celebration. But in the sixteenth century, Solomon Luria didn't like what he saw. In his commentary on the Talmud, he condemned bar mitzvah parties as "occasions for wild levity, just for the purpose of stuffing the gullet" (Yam Shel Shelomo, Baba Kama, 7:37).

The rabbis of the Middle Ages eventually enacted laws to limit spending on festivities. They did this to protect the dignity of the less wealthy.... The rabbis [also] worried about the jealousy of gentile neighbors, who might use displays of Jewish affluence as an excuse for a pogrom.... Finally, some historians suggest that these laws kept the emerging *nouveau riche* in their places so they did not threaten the status of the Jewish old guard. (*Putting God on the Guest List,* pp. 80–81)

Today we're going to talk about everyone's favorite subject—bar and bat mitzvah parties. Have any of you attended a particularly great bar/bat mitzvah celebration? A really terrible one?

Every so often in Jewish history, communities have made rules about celebration and how fancy or un-fancy those celebrations could be. Sometimes those laws were about the kinds of clothing that Jews could or could not wear. Here are a few examples.

Closing Question

Can synagogues make rules or guidelines about celebration? Do you think it would be fair for them to do so? How would it be handled—by the rabbi, groups of lay leaders, or as a joint project?

Sumptuary Laws

From Jacob Rader Marcus, *The Jew in the Medieval World: A Source Book, 315–1791*. New York: Hebrew Union College, revised edition, 2000.

From Forli, Italy
May 18, 1418

In order also to humble our hearts, and to walk modestly before our God, and not to show off in the presence of the Gentiles, we have agreed that from today … no Jew or Jewess of the above recorded Jewish community shall be so arrogant as to wear a fur-lined jacket, unless, of course, it is black. Also the sleeves must not be lined with silk, because that would be arrogant…. Likewise no woman shall openly wear a belt if its silver weighs more than ten ounces.

From Valladolid, Spain
May 2, 1432

No son of Israel of the age of fifteen or more shall wear any cloak of gold thread, olive-colored material or silk, or any cloak trimmed with gold or silk, nor a cloak with rich trimmings or gold cloth. This prohibition does not include the clothes worn at a time of festivity or at the reception of a lord or a lady, nor at balls or similar social occasions. Let various communities keep in mind that we are in dispersion because of our sins, and if they desire to establish more rigorous rules than this they have the power to do so.

Lithuania
September 4, 1637

With respect to banquets: Because people are spending too much money unnecessarily on festive meals, such as circumcisions and marriages, every Jewish community which has a rabbi is expected to assemble its officers and rabbi and to consider the number of guests which is suitable for every individual, in view of his wealth and the occasion, to invite to a festive meal.

Lithuania
1697

Young men and women, and particularly servants of both sexes, are not allowed to go to a dance at night without having been invited.

Questions for Discussion

1. What is the purpose of the rule from Forli? *(Teacher's Tip: To make Jews humble before others and God.)*

2. Why didn't the people who wrote this rule want Jews to show off in the presence of gentiles? *(Teacher's Tip: To avoid encouraging the stereotypes about Jewish wealth that persist to this day. Also, they feared mob violence and that taxes would be raised.)*

3. At what age does this rule imply that citizens of Valladolid became adults? *(Teacher's Tip: Fifteen, based on the restrictions imposed on people over that age.)*

4. What do you think this rule means by "a time of festivity"? *(Teacher's Tip: Holidays and life-cycle celebrations such as weddings, funerals, and—most likely—bar mitzvah parties.)*

5. Based on this rule, what kind of lives do you think Jews led in Spain at this time? Were the upper levels of society probably open to them? *(Teacher's Tip: Jews in Spain were very comfortable at that time—notice that the date is exactly sixty years before 1492, the expulsion. And if Jews weren't able to travel in the upper levels of society, this rule wouldn't have made an exception for a reception for "a lord or a lady." They're royalty!)*

6. What theological view does this law support? *(Teacher's Tip: That Jews are in dispersion—spread out around the world—because of their sins.)*

7. Do you think overspending on life-cycle and holiday celebrations was a big problem for Jews living in Lithuania in 1637? *(Teacher's Tip: To merit a rule like this, overspending was probably a* huge *problem. Think about Jewish society today: Some people have very expensive life-cycle celebrations, yet most synagogues don't restrict how much money can be spent throwing them or how many guests can attend.)*

8. Why might a rule have been made in 1697 prohibiting Lithuanian young people from going to parties or dances without being invited? *(Teacher's Tip: Because there was a lot of party crashing going on! Otherwise, it wouldn't have been something important enough to discuss, let alone to make or enforce a rule about.)*

7

To a Skeptical Jewish Parent

One day, the great writer Franz Kafka was strolling in a park in Berlin, when he saw a little girl crying because she had lost her doll. Kafka tried to comfort her, telling her that the doll had merely gone on a trip, and that he had just seen the doll and had spoken to it. The doll had promised Kafka that it would stay in touch with the girl and would send a letter to her from time to time. Whenever she would come to the park, Kafka said he would bring her a letter from the doll.

As you can imagine, Kafka himself wrote letters to the little girl, letting her think that the doll had written them. Eventually, he sent her a new doll. He told her that the new doll was the old doll but its appearance had changed since the last time she saw it because of the great adventures she had had.

The doll is a metaphor for religious faith. The old doll has indeed changed, just as we may not be able to reclaim the old, seemingly naive faith of our ancestors. But by struggling with our faith, we can reclaim a new belief for ourselves and for our children. (*Putting God on the Guest List*, pp. 92–93)

God on Trial

(An Activity for Parents and Kids)

Summary

By acting as jury in three cases in which God is the defendant, participants will be introduced to traditional Jewish views of God and struggle with their own ideas of God.

Before You Begin, You Need

- A room that could be made to resemble a courtroom. (There is nothing sacrilegious about doing this in a chapel or sanctuary.)
- Paper and a pencil or pen for each participant
- A copy of the three court cases on p. 39 for each participant
- A copy of the responses to evil and suffering on pp. 40–41 for each participant
- Courtroom paraphernalia, if desired. This could include a robe, a high desk, or gavel for the judge.

Doing the Activity

1. Read to the group the activity opening text on p. 38.

2. Appoint a teacher or the rabbi to act as the judge.

3. Appoint a bailiff, who will read aloud each case.

4. Distribute to each participant one copy of the cases on p. 39 and one copy of the responses to suffering on pp. 40–41.

5. Break the participants into three groups.

6. Assign one case to each group, who should then read its case.

7. Each group must divide into two teams: the prosecution (who will argue that God is responsible for the bad thing that happened) and the defense (who will argue that God isn't responsible).

8. Each team should discuss their case in the light of the Jewish responses to suffering on pp. 40–41. Group members should take notes.

9. A prosecutor, who will sum up the prosecution arguments, and a defense attorney, who will sum up the defense's case, should be appointed within each team.

10. The bailiff should read the first case. Then, the prosecutor assigned to this case should present the prosecution's case, as discussed by his or her group members. The defense attorney then rebuts, summing up his or her group's arguments that God is not responsible.

11. After each case, the judge should say: "I have no decision and there can be no sentence." There is no final answer when we are struggling with God issues.

12. This process should be repeated until each case has been argued.

13. Regroup and discuss the trials and some of the insights people shared during the activity.

14. Bring the activity to an end with a discussion of the closing question below.

Opening Words

Why do bad things happen to people, and why doesn't it seem that God cares when they do happen? Who can think of some times when they have thought about this? [Invite discussion.]

Struggling with and questioning God are two traditions repeated again and again in our sacred books—and our lives. Today we are going to engage in a very old and strange Jewish custom. We're going to put God on trial for three bad things that happened.

Closing Question

Bad things will always happen, and humanity will always try to figure out why. But even in the face of this uncertainty, Jews are guided by the *mitzvah* of *tikkun olam* ("repairing the world"), which tells us that we all must work to make the world a better place. Could you do anything to lessen someone else's suffering or make the world a better place?

God on Trial

Case One: The Death of Spiffy the Dog

Spiffy, the Schwartz family's cocker spaniel, was having a great afternoon of running around the yard, chasing bugs. Unfortunately, Sam Schwartz, age eight, left the gate open. This allowed Spiffy to run into the front yard and then onto the street.

By coincidence, Irving Cohen, age eighty-nine, was driving down the street. Mr. Cohen's eyesight is very good, but he is losing hearing in his right ear. That was the ear that could have heard Spiffy barking. Unfortunately, it did not. By the time Mr. Cohen braked, he had hit Spiffy. He felt terrible about it.

The Schwartz kids ran out into the street, sobbing. One of them said: "O God, how could You let this happen?"

Case Two: Francine, the Jock with the Pox

Francine Frank was fifteen years old. She was excited about a big softball game that was coming up. After all, she was the pitcher and the team depended on her.

But the day before the game, Francine noticed some spots on her stomach. "They're nothing," she said to herself. Wrong! Soon those spots migrated to her face. Uh-oh—she had measles! No one gets measles anymore. Except for Francine. Now she would have to miss the big game. Who knew how her team would do without her? Angry, she muttered to herself: "Thanks, God. Thanks a whole lot! Where were You when I needed You?"

Case Three: Terrible Todd's Sticky Fingers

It was bound to happen sooner or later. Todd Terrowitz, age thirteen, was finally caught shoplifting. In the past he had stolen candy bars at the local drug store, but Todd had worked his way up to CDs at the mall. He grabbed a bunch of CDs and shoved them into his pocket. Then the mall's plainclothes detective busted him. Todd had to go to juvenile court. Who knew what was going to happen to him there? As they were walking into the court, Todd's father said: "God, why are You doing this to me?"

Traditional Jewish Responses to Evil and Suffering

Fuhgetaboudit! You'll Never Get It!
(God said this to Job at the end of the Book of Job.)
- People can't understand God's ways.
- There is an ultimate purpose for suffering, known only by God. Humanity must have faith in God's justice.
- God's ways will be made understandable to us in the next world.

It's Your Fault
(Job's friends said this to him when he was suffering.)
- People are punished for their sins and failings.
- The sins of the fathers come back to the children.
- You get punished for the bad things you've done in this world, but you get rewarded for the good things you've done in the world to come.
- If you're suffering, it's because you sinned.

God Is Playing Peek-a-Boo with the World
(Job said this to his friends when he was suffering.)
- God is hiding the divine face—a temporary abandonment of the world, a suspension of God's active surveillance.

Other responses to suffering

- When permission is given to the angel of death to do its thing, the angel does not differentiate between the righteous and wicked.

- The righteous will get their reward in the world to come.

- The individual is punished along with the rest of the community for communal sin.

- *Yissurin shel ahavah* (suffering of love)—suffering is actually a good thing. It exists to purify, ennoble, and chasten humanity. It raises humanity to a higher level, tests humanity, and increases humanity's reward in the world to come.

- Suffering inspires people to reflect on their failures and to develop their potential.

- The process of divine justice takes time and humanity must have patience.

- Stuff happens—nature is morally neutral and every event isn't an act of judgment.

- God isn't active in the world in order to ensure humanity's freedom. That's why God doesn't jump in to save people anymore.

- Suffering pushes humanity over the brink to rise up against oppression and demand freedom.

- There is no reason why we suffer and there will never be one.

- Now we don't know why people suffer, but we will in the Messianic era.

8

The Shabbat Morning Worship Service: Finding Your Place in the Words

The Prayer Fair
(An Activity for Parents and Kids)

Summary

Traveling through the Shabbat morning service, participants will explore the meaning of some of its prayers.

Before You Begin, You Need

- Twelve "stations"—e.g., tables, desks, or other flat surfaces—each devoted to one of twelve prayers from the Shabbat morning service. Each station should be prepared with a copy of the appropriate prayer and prop, as outlined below. Prayers can be found in *Putting God on the Guest List*, 3rd Ed., on the page numbers as noted.

  Yotzer, found on pp. 108–109 of *Putting God on the Guest List*
  Prop: A flashlight. Turned on and off, it symbolizes light and darkness.

  Shema Yisrael, pp. 110–111
  Prop: Personal ads from a newspaper or magazine. The *Shema* is about a relationship with God, and these ads are from people who are looking for a relationship.

  Ve-ahavta, pp. 111–112
  Prop: A *mezuzah* or *tefilin.* These ritual objects are mentioned in the *Ve-ahavta.*

  Geulah, pp. 113–114
  Prop: A large bowl of water. This symbolizes the moment when the Israelites crossed the Sea of Reeds (also known as the Red Sea).

Avot, p. 115

Prop: Family pictures. *Avot* talks about our ancestors in the Bible. These biblical figures are our family members, just like the people in these snapshots.

Gevurot, pp. 116–117

Prop: Comic books featuring super heroes. In this prayer, God is described as being heroic. In fact, God is far more heroic than the super heroes in any comic book!

Kedusha, pp. 118–119

Prop: Pictures of angels. When we sing the *Kedusha,* we imagine ourselves soaring into the heavens with the angels, whom Jews believe to be invisible messengers of God.

Avodah, pp. 120–121

Prop: A picture of the Temple Mount or Western Wall in Jerusalem, or a diagram or sketch of the Second Temple. This prayer expresses hope that we feel as close to God as our ancestors felt when they prayed in the ancient Temple in Jerusalem. This photograph shows us what is left of the ancient Temple, destroyed by the Romans in the year 70 C.E. (Alternately, this diagram or sketch shows us what the Second Temple looked like.)

Birchat Shalom, pp. 122–123

Prop: A collage of headlines about places experiencing war or peace. This prayer asks for peace, a goal that often seems distant and impossible to realize.

Aleinu, pp. 123–125

Prop: A globe. *Aleinu* helps us dream about the time when the whole world turns to God alone. This doesn't mean that everyone will be Jewish. It means that if everyone believes in God, then people might treat each other better.

Kaddish, pp. 126–127

Prop: A *yahrzeit* candle. *Kaddish* reminds us of those who have died, just as this *yahrzeit* candle reminds us of the light that they brought into our lives.

• Enough paper and pencils or pens for each participant to take notes

• A copy of the questions for discussion on p. 45 for each participant

• Seats and drinks for Kiddush after the "service"

Doing the Activity

1. Read to the group the activity opening text below.

2. Break the participants into smaller groups.

3. Distribute copies of the questions for discussion on p. 45. The appropriate question should be considered as the groups encounter each new prayer.

4. Each group should discuss an opening question: When has a prayer experience deeply touched you?

5. When everyone in each group has answered the question, that group may begin to move through the fair.

6. Each group will travel from station to station. At each station groups should read the prayer, examine the artifact on the table, and discuss the connection between them. Before moving to a new station, each group should answer the appropriate discussion question from p. 45.

7. Once they have completed the prayer circuit, each group should join the Kiddush reception in honor of their successful prayer experience.

8. Bring the activity to an end with a discussion of the closing question below.

Opening Words

As Rabbi Henry Slonimsky ... once wrote: "I regard our old Jewish *siddur* [prayerbook] as the most important single Jewish book. It is a closer record of Jewish sufferings, Jewish needs, Jewish hopes and aspirations, than the Bible itself. If you want to know what Judaism is, you can find out by absorbing that book."

[Jewish ritual invites us to] perform a sacred drama that reflects our beliefs, our needs, our dreams, our values. (*Putting God on the Guest List*, p. 104)

The purpose of the Prayer Fair is to familiarize you with the Shabbat morning service so on bar/bat mitzvah day you can feel comfortable and participate in the service.

We will also be asking you to consider the deeper meanings of some of the prayers. It is our hope that you will continue to think about these meanings as you come to services in preparation for bar/bat mitzvah.

Closing Question

How is the Shabbat worship service like a journey? How is the *siddur* [prayerbook] like a roadmap? Did looking at these prayers today in a new way help you to develop a clearer understanding of them?

Questions for Discussion

Yotzer: What are some physical sources of light in our world? What are some spiritual sources of light? Name five people who you think are sources of light.

Shema Yisrael: The personal ads are for people who are lonely and would like a relationship. "Lonely" is an alternate translation of *echad,* a Hebrew word used in the *Shema* to mean "one." Are there some ways that we can keep God company?

Ve-ahavta: All the commands in this prayer are meant to remind us of one thing. What do you think that is?

Geulah: Give examples of times when you thought that all hope was lost, but you made it through anyway.

Avot: Tell stories about the way people in your family have lived their faith, or their own, special ways of being Jewish.

Gevurot: Do you think there's anything God can't do? If so, specify what and why.

Kedusha: Have there been any times in your life when you felt a sense of awe or "wow-ness"? When?

Avodah: Are there any specific places in Israel that you would like to visit? Why? What's special about them?

Birchat Shalom: What are some ways that you can contribute to peace in your family, your community, or even your world?

Aleinu: If everyone followed God's rules, how might the world be different?

Mourner's Kaddish: Talk about some famous people who have died: Martin Luther King Jr.; Pope John Paul II; Ilon Ramon, who died in the Columbia explosion; President Ronald Reagan; John Lennon of the Beatles; and others. How did they bring light into people's lives?

About Jewish Lights

People of all faiths and backgrounds yearn for books that attract, engage, educate, and spiritually inspire.

Our principal goal is to stimulate thought and help all people learn about who the Jewish People are, where they come from, and what the future can be made to hold. While people of our diverse Jewish heritage are the primary audience, our books speak to people in the Christian world as well and will broaden their understanding of Judaism and the roots of their own faith.

We bring to you authors who are at the forefront of spiritual thought and experience. While each has something different to say, they all say it in a voice that you can hear.

Our books are designed to welcome you and then to engage, stimulate, and inspire. We judge our success not only by whether or not our books are beautiful and commercially successful, but by whether or not they make a difference in your life.

For a complete list of all Jewish Lights books, request our catalog by calling us at (800) 962-4544, faxing to (802) 457-4004, or view it online at www.jewishlights.com.

Stuart M. Matlins, Publisher

The Book of Miracles   AWARD WINNER!
A Young Person's Guide to Jewish Spiritual Awareness
by Lawrence Kushner

For ages 9 & up

Introduces kids to a way of everyday spiritual thinking to last a lifetime. Kushner, whose award-winning books have brought spirituality to life for countless adults, now shows young people how to use Judaism as a foundation on which to build their lives.
6 x 9, 96 pp, HC, 2-color illus., ISBN 1-879045-78-8 **$16.95**

I Am Jewish
Personal Reflections Inspired by the Last Words of Daniel Pearl
Edited by Judea and Ruth Pearl

For all ages

Almost 150 Jews—both famous and not—from all walks of life, from all around the world, write about Identity, Heritage, Covenant / Chosenness and Faith, Humanity and Ethnicity, and *Tikkun Olam* and Justice.
6 x 9, 304 pp, Deluxe PB w/flaps, ISBN 1-58023-259-0 **$18.99**
Hardcover, ISBN 1-58023-183-7 **$24.99**
Download a free copy of the *I Am Jewish Teacher's Guide* at our website: www.jewishlights.com

The Story of the Jews
A 4,000-Year Adventure—A Graphic History Book
Written and illustrated by *Stan Mack*

For all ages

Through witty cartoons and accurate narrative, illustrates the major characters and events that have shaped the Jewish people and culture.
6 x 9, 304 pp, Quality PB, Illus., ISBN 1-58023-155-1 **$16.95**

Tough Questions Jews Ask
A Young Adult's Guide to Building a Jewish Life
By *Rabbi Edward Feinstein*

For ages 12 & up

Invites you to explore the difficult questions that are central to Jewish religious and spiritual life, and welcomes you to join the discussion that has helped shape what Judaism is today—and can be—in the future.
6 x 9, 160 pp, Quality PB, ISBN 1-58023-139-X **$14.99**   For ages 12 & up
   Also Available: **Tough Questions Jews Ask Teacher's Guide**
   8½ x 11, 72 pp, PB, ISBN 1-58023-187-X **$8.95**

Holidays/Holy Days

Leading the Passover Journey
The Seder's Meaning Revealed, the Haggadah's Story Retold
By Rabbi Nathan Laufer

Uncovers the hidden meaning of the Seder's rituals and customs.
6 x 9, 208 pp, Hardcover, ISBN 1-58023-211-6 **$24.99**

Reclaiming Judaism as a Spiritual Practice
Holy Days and Shabbat
By Rabbi Goldie Milgram

Provides a framework for understanding the powerful and often unexplained intellectual, emotional, and spiritual tools that are essential for a lively, relevant, and fulfilling Jewish spiritual practice. 7 x 9, 272 pp, Quality PB, ISBN 1-58023-205-1 **$19.99**

7th Heaven
Celebrating Shabbat with Rebbe Nachman of Breslov
By Moshe Mykoff with the Breslov Research Institute

Explores the art of consciously observing Shabbat and understanding in-depth many of the day's spiritual practices. 5⅛ x 8¼, 224 pp, Deluxe PB w/flaps, ISBN 1-58023-175-6 **$18.95**

The Women's Passover Companion
Women's Reflections on the Festival of Freedom
Edited by Rabbi Sharon Cohen Anisfeld, Tara Mohr and Catherine Spector

Groundbreaking. A provocative conversation about women's relationships to Passover as well as the roots and meanings of women's seders.
6 x 9, 352 pp, Hardcover, ISBN 1-58023-128-4 **$24.95**

The Women's Seder Sourcebook
Rituals & Readings for Use at the Passover Seder
Edited by Rabbi Sharon Cohen Anisfeld, Tara Mohr and Catherine Spector

Gathers the voices of more than one hundred women in readings, personal and creative reflections, commentaries, blessings, and ritual suggestions that can be incorporated into your Passover celebration. 6 x 9, 384 pp, Hardcover, ISBN 1-58023-136-5 **$24.95**

Creating Lively Passover Seders: *A Sourcebook of Engaging Tales, Texts & Activities*
By David Arnow, Ph.D. 7 x 9, 416 pp, Quality PB, ISBN 1-58023-184-5 **$24.99**

Hanukkah, 2nd Edition: *The Family Guide to Spiritual Celebration*
By Dr. Ron Wolfson. Edited by Joel Lurie Grishaver.
7 x 9, 240 pp, illus., Quality PB, ISBN 1-58023-122-5 **$18.95**

The Jewish Family Fun Book: *Holiday Projects, Everyday Activities, and Travel Ideas with Jewish Themes* *By Danielle Dardashti and Roni Sarig. Illus. by Avi Katz.*
6 x 9, 288 pp, 70+ b/w illus. & diagrams, Quality PB, ISBN 1-58023-171-3 **$18.95**

The Jewish Gardening Cookbook: *Growing Plants & Cooking for Holidays & Festivals*
By Michael Brown 6 x 9, 224 pp, 30+ illus., Quality PB, ISBN 1-58023-116-0 **$16.95**

The Jewish Lights Book of Fun Classroom Activities: *Simple and Seasonal Projects for Teachers and Students* *By Danielle Dardashti and Roni Sarig*
6 x 9, 240 pp, Quality PB, ISBN 1–58023–206–X **$19.99**

Passover, 2nd Edition: *The Family Guide to Spiritual Celebration*
By Dr. Ron Wolfson with Joel Lurie Grishaver
7 x 9, 352 pp, Quality PB, ISBN 1-58023-174-8 **$19.95**

Shabbat, 2nd Edition: *The Family Guide to Preparing for and Celebrating the Sabbath*
By Dr. Ron Wolfson 7 x 9, 320 pp, illus., Quality PB, ISBN 1-58023-164-0 **$19.95**

Sharing Blessings: *Children's Stories for Exploring the Spirit of the Jewish Holidays*
By Rahel Musleah and Michael Klayman
8½ x 11, 64 pp, Full-color illus., Hardcover, ISBN 1-879045-71-0 **$18.95**
For ages 6 & up

Order Form

Check enclosed for $_____ payable to
Jewish Lights Publishing
or
Charge my credit card: ❏ VISA ❏ MASTERCARD

Card # _____

Exp. date_____ CID#_____

Signature _____

Name _____ Phone_____

Street _____

City / State / Zip_____

Discount Schedule for Quantity Orders	
Copies of the <u>SAME</u> book	Discount
3–6	10%
7–14	20%
15–24	25%
25–49	30%
50+	35%

#Book	Title	ISBN	Price	Total
____	_____	_____	$ _____	$ _____
____	_____	_____	$ _____	$ _____
____	_____	_____	$ _____	$ _____
____	_____	_____	$ _____	$ _____

Minus Discount_____% <$_____>

Subtotal $_____

Shipping and handling (Add $3.95 for the first book, $2.00 ea. add'l book to a maximum of $20.00) $_____

TOTAL $_____

Or phone, fax, mail or e-mail to: **JEWISH LIGHTS Publishing**
Sunset Farm Offices, Route 4 • P.O. Box 237 • Woodstock, Vermont 05091
Tel: (802) 457-4000 • Fax: (802) 457-4004 • www.jewishlights.com
Credit card orders: (800) 962-4544 (8:30AM–5:30PM ET Monday–Friday)
Generous discounts on quantity orders. SATISFACTION GUARANTEED. Prices subject to change.